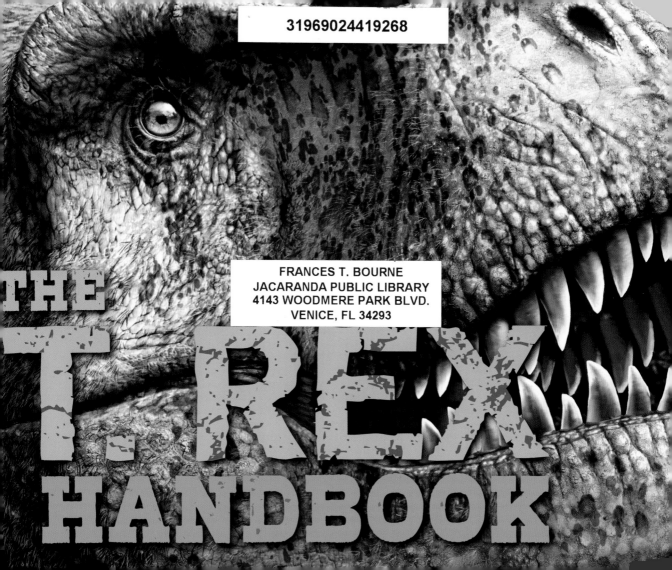

THE T. REX HANDBOOK

The T. rex Handbook
Abridged from Prehistoric Predators

13-Digit ISBN: 978-1604336030
10-Digit ISBN: 160433603X

This book may be ordered by mail from the publisher. Please include $5.95 for postage and handling.
Please support your local bookseller first!

Books published by Cider Mill Press Book Publishers are available at special discounts for bulk purchases in the United States by corporations, institutions, and other organizations. For more information, please contact the publisher.

Applesauce Press is an imprint of Cider Mill Press Book Publishers
"Where good books are ready for press"
PO Box 454, 12 Spring Street
Kennebunkport, Maine 04046

Visit us on the Web!
www.cidermillpress.com

Cover and interior design by Shelby Newsted
Typography: Destroy, Gipsiero, PMN Caecilia, Block Berthold

Image Credits:
Photographs on pages 18 and 21 used under license from Shutterstock.
Illustrations on pages 16, 25, 28, and 42 used under license from Shutterstock.
Vector silhouettes on pages 9, 10, 11, 12, 13, 15, 16, 17, 19, 20, 23, 25, 27, 29, 31, 33, 42, 45, 52, 53, 54, 56, and 58 used under license from Shutterstock.
All other artwork by Julius T. Csotonyi.

Printed in China

1 2 3 4 5 6 7 8 9 0
Derivative Edition

THE T. REX HANDBOOK

BRIAN SWITEK • ILLUSTRATED BY JULIUS CSOTONYI

APPLESAUCE PRESS

Kennebunkport, ME

TABLE OF CONTENTS

Tyrannosaurus rex

WHO WAS T. REX?

Tyrannosaurus rex means "king of the tyrant lizards." And that title fits! Some dinosaurs were just as big, and some were stranger-looking, but *T. rex* was the ultimate prehistoric predator.

HOW LONG DID T. REX LIVE FOR?

EGGS: We actually don't know what a T. *rex* egg looked like, because none have been discovered yet. Maybe you'll be the first one to find an egg!

BABY *T. REX*: Hatchlings might have been born with fuzzy feathers, like birds. These would have helped keep them warm while they grew up.

YOUNG (JUVENILE) *T. REX*: Young *T. rex* looked very different from their parents. They had long legs, a narrow snout, and a few extra teeth!

ADULT *T. REX*: It took a *T. rex* about 20 years to grow to adult size. The oldest one of these dinosaurs ever found was about 30 years old.

WHAT WERE T. REX EYES LIKE?

The T. *rex* had binocular-like vision, which most predators alive today have. They could see an object 13 times more clearly than a human, and they had good depth perception! It helps that each T. *rex* eyeball was nearly as big as a softball!

Oddly enough, the color of T. *rex* eyes is unknown.

Tyrannosaurus rex

HOW POWERFUL WAS THE T. REX BITE?

T. *rex* had one of the most powerful bites of all time and was famous for its enormous jaws. It could bite down over 47 times harder than you!

That's three times greater than a great white shark!

18

HOW SHARP WERE T. REX TEETH?

Tyrannosaurus rex could ram its teeth into prey hard enough to cut through the toughest dinosaur hides. This ability made T. *rex* a deadly hunter. And we know from studying fossilized *Tyrannosaurus rex* poop that they ate both flesh and bone. T. *rex*'s neck muscles were also extremely strong.

HOW BIG WAS A T. REX SKULL?

The largest *T. rex* skull on record was discovered in the 1960s...

IT WAS 59 INCHES LONG!

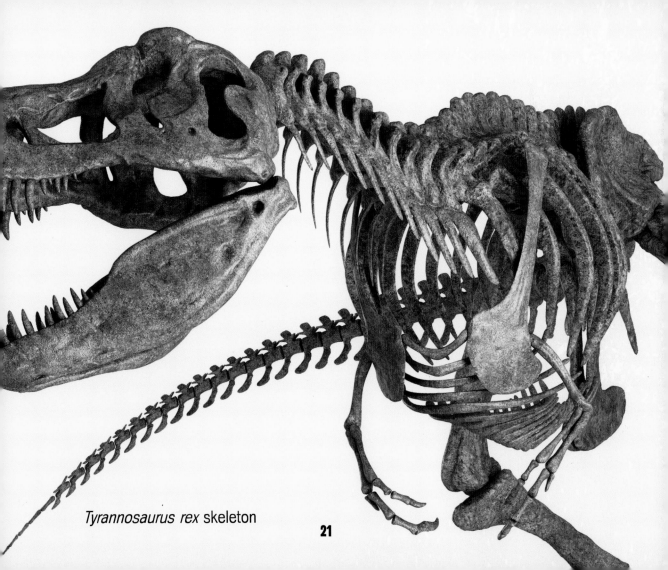

Tyrannosaurus rex skeleton

21

WHY DID T. REX HAVE SUCH LITTLE ARMS?

T. rex had tiny, two-fingered arms, but no one really knows why they were so tiny. Compared to your arms, though, they were really strong! One study suggests they could lift over 400 pounds. That's like picking up a bear or a gorilla!

HOW FAST COULD T. REX RUN?

UP TO 25 MILES PER HOUR!

Because T. rex was so big and had a long tail, it couldn't turn very quickly—it took about two seconds for the dinosaur to turn—or run very fast. It could only reach 25 mph. That's slower than your family's car on the highway or an ostrich, but still faster than you can sprint!

Tyrannosaurus rex

25

UP TO 100 MPH

UP TO 45 MPH

UP TO 25 MPH

HOW DID T. REX BALANCE?

Because of its large skull, T. rex had to have a thick tail to balance it out. We used to think that T. rex stood upright with its tail on the ground, but we recently figured out their tails were in the air and level with their heads! This is made running and hunting easier for T. rex.

HOW BIG WAS T. REX?

T. rex was the largest of the Tyrannosaurids. They could grow up to 40 feet long (half as long as a blue whale!) and as tall as a giraffe.

They could weigh up to 9 tons. That's more than an African Elephant or 3 hippos!

40 FEET LONG

20 FEET TALL

5 FEET, 9 INCHES

Tyrannosaurus rex

29

30

WHAT DID T. REX EAT?

Tyrannosaurus rex was likely both a hunter and a scavenger, never passing up a meal. They could kill prey by shaking their heads from side to side and ripping apart carcasses. They could even throw a 110-pound chunk of meat 15 feet into the air and catch it again. To a T. *rex*, you'd be just a quick bite.

WHEN DID T. REX LIVE?

TIMELINE

PERMIAN PERIOD	TRIASSIC PERIOD	JURASSIC PERIOD	CRETACEOUS PERIOD	PALEOCENE PERIOD
299–252 MILLION YEARS AGO	252–201 MILLION YEARS AGO	201–145 MILLION YEARS AGO	145–66 MILLION YEARS AGO	66–56 MILLION YEARS AGO

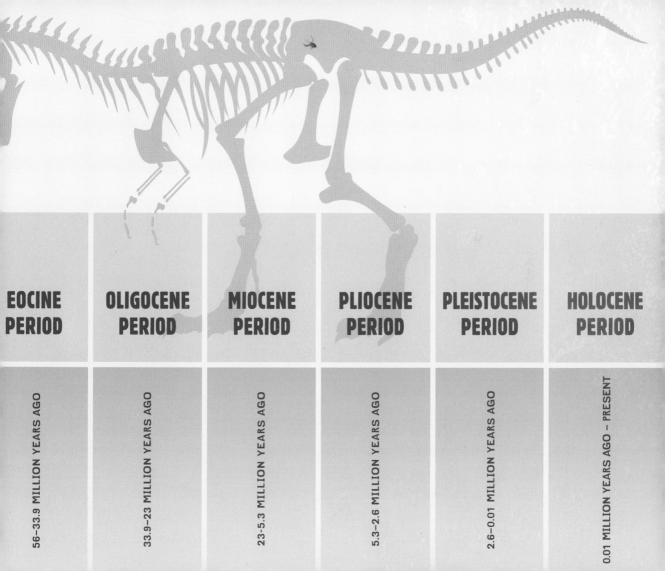

EOCINE PERIOD

56–33.9 MILLION YEARS AGO

OLIGOCENE PERIOD

33.9–23 MILLION YEARS AGO

MIOCENE PERIOD

23–5.3 MILLION YEARS AGO

PLIOCENE PERIOD

5.3–2.6 MILLION YEARS AGO

PLEISTOCENE PERIOD

2.6–0.01 MILLION YEARS AGO

HOLOCENE PERIOD

0.01 MILLION YEARS AGO – PRESENT

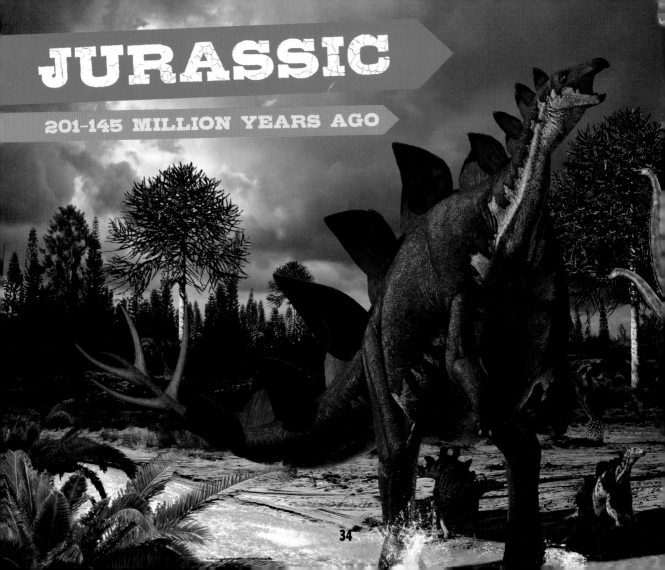

JURASSIC

201-145 MILLION YEARS AGO

JURASSIC PERIOD

201–145 MILLION YEARS AGO

You may think the **TYRANNOSAURUS REX** lived during this period, but it didn't. However, many other awesome predators roamed the earth at this time.

An early Jurassic dinosaur was **DILOPHOSAURUS**. It had a pair of thin crests running along its head.

Its cousin **CRYOLOPHOSAURUS** showed off differently, with a cockscomb sticking up over its eyes.

ALLOSAURUS was an even bigger dinosaur that had a triangular horn over each eye.

No one knows why these predators looked this way, but these features might have helped the dinosaurs recognize each other or impress potential mates.

Crylophosaurus

CRETACEOUS

145-66 MILLION YEARS AGO

CRETACEOUS PERIOD

145-66 MILLION YEARS AGO

The Jurassic period was only the beginning of the dinosaurs' rule. They also reigned during the Cretaceous period. The Cretaceous period lasted for 79 million years. But dinosaurs didn't stay the same for all those years—they evolved into amazing and sometimes frightening new forms!

During this time, there was the **ACROCANTHOSAURUS**, a dinosaur with hooked hand claws and a ridge on its back.

There was also the sail-backed **SPINOSAURUS**.

Later, other dinosaurs evolved, including **GIGANOTOSAURUS** —a relative of **ACROCANTHOSAURUS**—and, of course, the great **TYRANNOSAURUS**.

Giganotosaurus carolinii

Adult and juvenile *Tyrannosaurus rex*

MEET THE T. REX
FAMILY

Tyrannosauroids (family of *T. rex* and its relatives) weren't always the biggest predators in their areas. The first ones were small! But they grew to become some of the largest carnivores ever.

GUANLONG WUCAII

GWAN-long

SIZE: Almost 10 feet long

AGE: About 160 million years ago

PHYSICAL PROFILE: A small tyrannosaur with long arms, a shallow skull, and a crest jutting from its face.

SCIENCE BITE: The first skeleton of *Guanlong* was found in a huge mud hole made by the footprint of a long-necked sauropod dinosaur.

When we think of *Tyrannosaurus rex*, we imagine giant meat-eaters with huge heads and tiny arms. But some of T. *rex*'s earliest relatives were surprisingly small. *Guanlong* was a T. *rex* relative during the Jurassic period. It was a dinosaur with long arms, a short snout, a crest on its head, and a coat of dinofuzz on its body. It was only much later, during the Cretaceous period, that T. *rex*'s relatives became the most powerful creatures around.

GORGOSAURUS LIBRATUS

GORE-go-SAWR-us

SIZE: Up to 30 feet long

AGE: 76–75 million years ago

PHYSICAL PROFILE: A sleek, nimble tyrannosaur with a shallow skull and small horns above the eyes.

SCIENCE BITE: Young *Gorgosaurus* could pack on the pounds. During its teenage years, *Gorgosaurus* could gain over 110 pounds each year!

This *T. rex* relative had long legs that made it an agile hunter. But *Gorgosaurus* regularly scavenged for food, too. Thanks to its powerful sense of smell, *Gorgosaurus* was able to sniff out rotting meat—like this decaying mosasaur— as well as live prey. Tyrannosaurs like *Gorgosaurus* hunted and gathered to keep their strength up.

46

DASPLETOSAURUS TOROSUS

DAS-pleet-uh-SAWR-us

SIZE: Up to 30 feet long and 2.7 tons

AGE: 77–74 million years ago

PHYSICAL PROFILE: A big, heavily built tyrannosaur with a more powerful bite than its relative *Gorgosaurus*.

SCIENCE BITE: Some *Daspletosaurus* skulls have healed bite marks from wounds made by other tyrannosaurs. When these dinosaurs fought, they went right for the face!

Daspletosaurus was one of the largest and most impressive predators of the Cretaceous period. But why did they have such small arms? Paleontologists are not sure, but one guess was that they used their arms to push themselves off the ground after napping. Another idea is that as tyrannosaurs evolved, they caught prey with their jaws more and didn't use their arms as much. But even though their arms were very small, they still had some pretty strong muscles.

ALBERTOSAURUS SARCOPHAGUS

al-BER-tuh-SAWR-us

SIZE: Up to 30 feet long and 1.9 tons

AGE: 70 million years ago

PHYSICAL PROFILE: A large, sleek tyrannosaur with a big skull and tiny arms but more agility than the beefier *T. rex*

SCIENCE BITE: Meat-eating dinosaurs are often shown fighting with giant plant-eating dinosaurs. But the truth is, even the biggest carnivores probably hunted smaller dinosaurs.

Here, an *Albertosaurus* is trying to chomp down on a baby Spinops while the infant's parent tries to drive the *Albertosaurus* away. Infant dinosaurs, as well as those too old or sick to defend themselves, were much easier targets than healthy, adult dinosaurs. This may be why we don't have many fossils of infant dinosaurs.

50

51

"Black Beauty" has dark bones from the minerals in the surrounding rock during fossilization. It was found in 1980 near Crowsnest Pass, Alberta, Canada!

Barnum Brown found two partial skeletons: one in eastern Wyoming in 1900 and another in 1902 in Montana.

The first T. rex fossils ever found were dug up near Golden, Colorado in 1874.

A T. rex tooth was found near Deming, New Mexico, close to the Mexican border.

"Scotty" was discovered in 1991 and was the first one to be found in Saskatchewan!

The "Wankel" skeleton was found by Kathy Wankel in eastern Montana in 1989-1990. It was 38-feet long, and weighed 7 tons.

"Stan," a 65% complete specimen, was found near Buffalo, South Dakota in 1987.

Thanks to Stan, five more T. rex fossils were found near the Montana/South Dakota border in 2000.

"Sue" was found in South Dakota in 1990, by Sue Hendrickson, and was nearly 85% complete.

MAP KEY

U.S. State where a *T. rex* fossil has been found

Canadian province where a *T. rex* fossil has been found

52

WHERE HAVE FOSSILS BEEN FOUND?

From Saskatchewan, Canada to northern Mexico!

TRUE OR FALSE

Can you answer these questions about *T. rex*?

1. **T/F** Leaves and grass were T. *rex*'s favorite foods.

2. **T/F** It could bite down harder than a great white shark.

3. **T/F** T. *rex* eggs were green and shaped like chicken eggs.

4. **T/F** T. *rex* ate both flesh and bone.

5. **T/F** The *Spinosaurus* was a relative of T. *rex*.

Spinosaurus aegyptiacus

55

TRUE OR FALSE

Can you answer these questions about *T. rex*?

6. **T**/**F** It could weigh more than an African Elephant.

7. **T**/**F** T. *rex* fossils have been found in Canada.

8. **T**/**F** T. *rex* lived during the Jurassic period, like the movie!

9. **T**/**F** T. *rex* can run faster than the average human.

10. **T**/**F** *Tyrannosaurus rex* means "King of the Dinosaurs."

Allosaurus fragilis

About the Author

Brian Switek is a science writer and fossil fanatic. In addition to his books for adults—*Written in Stone* and *My Beloved Brontosaurus*—he blogs for *National Geographic*, hosts the short film series "Dinologue," and volunteers with museums and universities to discover new fossils across the American West. He lives in Utah.

About the Illustrator

Julius Csotonyi is one of the world's most high-profile and talented contemporary paleoartists. His considerable academic expertise informs his stunning, dynamic art. He has created life-sized dinosaur murals for the Royal Ontario Museum and for the Dinosaur Hall at the Natural History Museum of Los Angeles County as well as most of the artwork for the new Hall of Paleontology at the Houston Museum of Natural Science. He lives in Canada.

About Applesauce Press
What kid doesn't love Applesauce!

Good ideas ripen with time. From seed to harvest, Applesauce Press crafts books with beautiful designs, creative formats, and kid-friendly information on a variety of topics. Like our parent company, Cider Mill Press Book Publishers, our press bears fruit twice a year, publishing a new crop of titles each spring and fall.

"Where Good Books Are Ready for Press"

Visit us on the web at
www.cidermillpress.com
or write to us at
PO Box 454
12 Spring Street
Kennebunkport, ME 04046